BECOMING ONE

How GOD Preserved Our Covenant

BY
Earl Amis Hudson Jr.

PUBLISHER: HUDSON LEGACY PRESS
Atlanta, Georgia

HUDSON LEGACY
PRESS
"THE BLESSING
IS IN THE CLEANUP"

BECOMING ONE

How GOD Preserved Our Covenant

Published by Hudson Legacy Press
Atlanta, Georgia

eBook ISBN: 979-8-9936312-2-6
Print ISBN: 979-8-9936312-3-3

This book is a work of nonfiction.

Printed in the United States of America

Dedication

This book is dedicated to four women whose love, wisdom, and presence have profoundly influenced both of our lives and strengthened our marriage.

To Mrs. Linda, my oldest sister, whose love and honesty shaped my journey, and who embraced Tameka not only as family but as a true friend.

To Ms. Lottie, Tameka's mother, whose nurturing spirit and steady wisdom not only formed her daughter but also spoke into my life at the right time, calling me to reflection and change.

To Ms. Alice, my mother, whose example, discipline, and faith laid a foundation in me, and whose voice carried through my brother, confronted me with truth and responsibility.

To Mrs. Diane, my stepmother, who has always loved me unconditionally and whose love and acceptance were evident from the very beginning, I express my deepest gratitude for welcoming Tameka into our family and showing her genuine friendship.

To those who are now asleep in JESUS, your legacy lives on in us. And to the one still with us, we remain grateful for your continued love and presence. We honor what GOD has done through each of you and hold to the promise that one day, we will all be together again.

Foreword

Our love story is not conventional. It does not follow a Hollywood script for actors to portray on the big screen. It does not match the dreams of a young girl playing with her dolls, imagining herself as a bride and mother. Neither does it mirror the stories told in romance novels.

Our love story is real.

It is the story of two people longing for understanding, support, patience, and kindness—things we both felt were missing in our first marriages. We entered this relationship willing to go the distance, determined to give our all to each other...forever.

Did we make mistakes along the way? Absolutely. We did not always make the best decisions for our marriage or our family. But GOD.

I am so grateful that I serve a GOD who knew we would fall short, yet still made provision for us through His Word. In Paul's letter to the Corinthians, we are given a clear picture of what love truly is—and what it is not. Love requires surrender. It calls us beyond our selfish desires and invites us into something greater. And in the end, we are reminded of this truth: love never fails.

The scripture from 1 Corinthians 13:4–8 was our wedding Scripture. What I did not realize then was how deeply we would be tested in nearly every part of it. There were moments when we were not patient or kind. There were times when we were prideful, easily angered, and kept a record of wrongs. But GOD. Through it all, we are still here, standing together.

I never doubted that Earl was meant to be my husband. GOD made that clear to me, even during some of the most difficult seasons of our marriage. What I experienced during those moments was confirmation of something He had already spoken to me when I was 19 years old—that I would marry a minister.

Still, unresolved trauma found its way into our relationship, and we found ourselves in a fight for our lives. What I did not understand at the time was that this fight was not only about our marriage—it was about my healing too. Counseling and recovery programs became tools GOD used to restore what was broken.

What makes our relationship what it is today is our willingness to be uncomfortable. We chose to open our hearts to one another and confront the parts of ourselves most people avoid. We talked about the pain, the trauma, and the broken places we carried from our past. We allowed ourselves to be vulnerable so that we could heal—together.

We have worked through wounds from our childhoods. We have forgiven each other for the mistakes made during our marriage. We have apologized to our children for what they witnessed, and we have learned how to extend grace —not just in words, but in how we live.

Paul reminds us that no matter how gifted or accomplished we may be, without love, we have nothing. The greatest of all things is love—the kind of love that reflects CHRIST's love for us. That is the love we continue to grow into.

We may not be the model for marriage, and that is okay. Our marriage is ours—marked by imperfections, mistakes, growth, and grace. Our journey has been one of self-discovery, maturity, and deeper awareness. Looking back, I can see that every part of it was necessary. GOD has stripped away the old and clothed us in something new.

Today, we lead with grace and kindness, and our love reflects who GOD created us to be.

We are two imperfect people who, by GOD's grace, are perfect for each other.

In this book, Earl shares our story from his perspective—the good, the bad, and the difficult. Some may judge the choices we made, and that is to be expected. But what I know is this: GOD is a Redeemer. He renews minds, restores hearts, and transforms lives when we seek Him, confess, and turn back to Him.

This is a story of redemption—of love, hurt, betrayal, and forgiveness. And through it all, we give GOD the glory.

What you will read in these pages is only a portion of what we have lived through. My prayer is that as you read, you will see how GOD can truly transform a life from the inside out.

Tameka Hudson
Lithonia, GA

Introduction: Brokenness to Grace

When people see a marriage that has lasted for many years, they often assume it was built on constant harmony, natural compatibility, or some secret that made love easier. What they usually do not see are the years of learning, the difficult conversations, the disappointments, the misunderstandings, the growth, and the daily decision to remain committed when love requires more than emotion. From the outside, a long marriage can appear settled and secure, but what appears steady today was shaped over time through seasons of joy, failure, grace, truth, grief, recovery, and rebuilding.

This book is about a covenant shared by two people, but I can only truthfully tell the part of the story that belongs to me. Some of what happened between Tameka and me can only be understood through both of our perspectives, but her story is hers to tell. My responsibility is to speak honestly about what was revealed within me, the choices I made, the lessons I learned, and the grace GOD extended to us along the way.

Our marriage did not begin with two people who had everything figured out. It began with two people who loved each other, made a covenant, and stepped into that covenant carrying more than either of us understood. We were sincere, but sincerity is not the same as maturity. We were committed, but commitment alone does not automatically produce wisdom. Looking back now, I can see that I brought into our marriage patterns, assumptions, insecurities, and unresolved issues that would eventually test everything I believed about love, faith, responsibility, and covenant.

Before many of the struggles described in this book came to light, I was serving in ministry and preaching regularly. I had spent years studying Scripture, teaching others, and helping people navigate their own spiritual journeys. From the outside, my life appeared stable. I loved GOD, believed His Word, and sincerely wanted to live faithfully. Yet spiritual knowledge and spiritual health are not always the same thing. A person can understand truth and still avoid the parts of themselves that truth is trying to expose. There were areas of my life where I had understanding without full surrender, conviction without consistency, and knowledge without the deeper self-awareness that genuine transformation requires.

Even after my salvation and after answering the call to ministry, there were things within me I had not learned how to examine honestly. I believed many of my struggles were connected primarily to circumstances, relationships, stress, or seasons of life. What I did not understand was that some of the patterns shaping my responses had been present long before I recognized them. I understood sin theologically, but I did not yet understand how deeply certain desires, insecurities, emotional habits, and ways of thinking could continue influencing a person beneath the surface. I wanted to live differently, but wanting change and understanding the deeper work required for change are not always the same thing. Much of what affected me spiritually and emotionally remained hidden beneath routine, responsibility, ministry, and the appearance of stability.

What I could not see was that some things do not disappear simply because they remain dormant. Life can feel manageable for years before circumstances expose what was never fully addressed. Years later, I would discover that some of the most significant battles in my life had been forming long before I recognized them.

This book is not an attempt to justify the choices I made, nor is it an effort to soften the reality of what happened. It is an honest account of what was revealed once the covenant began exposing parts of me that had remained unexamined. Marriage has a way of bringing to the surface things that can remain unnoticed for years. It reveals strengths, weaknesses, assumptions, fears, expectations, and patterns that might otherwise stay concealed. What was revealed in our marriage did not leave either of us untouched. What I am accountable for is my own story, my own choices, and my own growth. That is the story I intend to tell honestly.

With time, I began to recognize things I could not see clearly in those earlier years. There were moments when I knew I was wrong and continued anyway. There were other moments when I refused to acknowledge what was happening because confronting it would have required truths I was not yet prepared to face. Some decisions should have been made sooner. Some conversations should have happened earlier. Some choices carried consequences that reached far beyond what I anticipated. Yet despite everything, our marriage did not collapse. Looking back now, I can see that something was sustaining us even when I could not fully recognize it.

At the time, I did not understand that grace was already at work. I assumed grace would arrive after the lessons had been learned and after the problems had been solved. What I eventually discovered was that GOD often begins working long before we recognize His presence. CHRIST was not waiting for me to fix myself before extending grace. He was meeting me in the middle of my brokenness, exposing what needed to be confronted and sustaining what might otherwise not have survived.

While GOD was dealing with me, Tameka was walking her own journey of faith, endurance, growth, and perseverance. We were not carrying the same responsibilities, nor were we facing the same questions, but neither of us would remain unchanged by what followed. Some of those changes would take years to recognize. Others would only become visible when we looked back and realized how differently we related to one another than we had before.

If you have read *Lessons From Ms. Alice*, then you already know something about the foundation on which I was raised. My mother taught discipline, responsibility, consistency, order, and perseverance through her words and her example. Those lessons were genuine, and they shaped me in meaningful ways. That is why one question became impossible for me to avoid: If I learned those lessons so well, how did I still make the choices I made?

The answer is not complicated, although it is uncomfortable. Learning a lesson is not the same as living it. Truth can be understood intellectually long before it becomes fully integrated into a person's life. What is known is not always practiced, and what is not practiced will eventually be tested. My failures were not evidence that my mother's lessons were wrong. They revealed the distance between what I had learned and what I had fully lived.

Over time, I also came to understand that becoming one is not confined to a wedding ceremony. A ceremony marks a covenant, but a covenant must be lived into over time. Marriage does not automatically refine character. More often, it reveals character. What is eventually revealed demands attention, and what is honestly confronted opens the possibility for change. Much of this book is about that process. It is about what happened when responsibility could no longer be avoided and when recovery, grace, and truth began reshaping what neither of us fully understood at the beginning.

Some parts of this story are mine alone, and I will discuss them openly. Other parts belong to Tameka, and I will speak of them only with care and respect. Where responsibility is mine, I will take it honestly. Where growth was shared, I will speak carefully and respectfully. My goal is not to assign blame or settle old accounts. My goal is to tell the truth about what happened and about the work GOD did through it.

If you have ever begun something out of order, justified something that later required confrontation, struggled with parts of yourself you did not fully understand, or discovered that love does not remove brokenness but often exposes it, then you may recognize parts of your own story in these pages. The details may differ, but the experience of confronting what has been hidden is one that many people understand.

One of the lessons that took me the longest to appreciate came from something my mother often said: "The blessing is in the cleanup." As a child, I thought she was talking about dishes, laundry, trash, and keeping a house in order. Years later, I realized her words reached far beyond household chores. Life has a way of creating messes that cannot be ignored forever. Relationships do as well. Cleanup requires honesty. It requires responsibility. It requires the willingness to face what has been avoided rather than pretending it does not exist. The blessing is not found in the mess itself. It is found in the willingness to confront the truth and participate in the work required to address it.

What follows is the story of a marriage tested, a man forced to confront himself, a woman who demonstrated more strength than I fully understood at the time, and a GOD whose grace proved greater than either of us could see during the most difficult seasons of our lives. It is the story of becoming one—not all at once, not without failure, and not without struggle, but through years of truth, growth, recovery, grace, and the ongoing work of learning how to live faithfully within a covenant.

The story is still being written.

PART I – BEFORE WE KNEW WHAT WE WERE CARRYING

Love often begins with hope before it fully understands what each person brings into the covenant. Before Tameka and I made our vows, our lives were already shaped by past experiences, family histories, sincere intentions, and choices that would later require deeper reflection.

These early chapters trace the beginning of our journey together: the circumstances that brought us close, the relationships that slowly began to heal, the day we made our vows, and the early years of blending our family. At the time, we believed love, commitment, and faith would carry us forward. In many ways, they did, but beneath the surface, there were still patterns, assumptions, and unresolved places we did not yet know how to name.

Chapter 1: Before the Vows

The relationship between Tameka and me did not begin on holy ground. We met while I was still married. Looking back, I do not believe my divorce was in keeping with what CHRIST taught about marriage, and I take full responsibility for the choices I made during that season of my life. At the time, I was not man enough to sit down with my wife and honestly tell her that I wanted a divorce. In my mind, the marriage was already over. Instead of addressing the situation directly, I allowed my actions to speak for me, and a physical separation followed shortly afterward, even though the divorce itself would take much longer to become final.

At the same time, I was serving in ministry. I preached, taught, and spent much of my time helping others navigate their spiritual lives. From the outside, my life appeared stable. I was working, serving, and carrying responsibilities that suggested everything was moving in the right direction. Yet I was also living outside of GOD's will in ways I was not honestly confronting. Looking back, I realize that serving GOD and obeying GOD are not always the same thing. Appearances can hide a great deal.

Tameka and I met during that season. She was involved in ministry, and our paths crossed naturally through church life and the work we were both doing. What began between us was not something either of us set out to pursue. There were no dramatic declarations or carefully planned intentions. It developed gradually, which made it easier to justify and harder to confront honestly.

One afternoon, Tameka came by my office for something related to ministry. It was an ordinary day by all appearances. But when I opened the door and looked into her eyes, I kissed her.

Even now, I can still remember that moment.

At the time, it did not seem life-changing. It was an amazing feeling, but I convinced myself it was simply that—an unexpected moment and a powerful emotion. I thought it was something I could dismiss if I chose not to examine it too closely. What I understand now is that moments rarely stay small when they are not confronted honestly. What began that day gradually became something more.

The truth is that I had already convinced myself my first marriage was ending. Because I believed the outcome was already decided, I allowed myself to excuse choices that I knew were wrong. At the time, I thought I was being honest with myself. Looking back, I can see that I was simply justifying what I wanted.

As time passed, Tameka and I grew closer. Conversation came easily between us. We laughed together, shared our faith, and found common ground in the things that mattered most. She understood parts of me that I often struggled to explain, and I felt understood in ways that were deeply meaningful. What had begun as an attraction increasingly felt like a future we were moving toward together.

As our relationship deepened, we became emotionally and physically involved. Neither of us was confused about the reality of what was happening. We knew our relationship had begun before my divorce was final, and we understood that the situation was not what it should have been.

Eventually, the divorce became final.

At the time, I believed that closing one chapter would automatically bring peace to the next. I thought that once the legal process was over, much of the tension surrounding my life would disappear. What I did not yet understand was that some things follow us into the future because they have never been honestly confronted.

Even so, life kept moving.

Tameka and I continued moving forward together, believing we were building a future that would leave the complications of the past behind us. Conversation came easily, our faith connected us, and the plans we made together increasingly centered on a shared future. As we talked about marriage, I believed we were moving toward something steady. I thought the hardest parts were behind us. I believed that once we stood before GOD, exchanged vows, and started our life together, everything that had been complicated would finally settle into place.

Not everyone around me saw things the way I did.

One Sunday evening, I was standing at the front of the church preparing to welcome a visiting women's ministry. Among the women arriving that evening was my oldest sister, Linda.

Linda had always been one of my strongest supporters. She believed in my calling, encouraged my ministry, and rarely hesitated to tell me the truth when she thought I needed to hear it. She also knew about my divorce, my relationship with Tameka, and the timing of everything that had happened.

When we came face to face that evening, neither of us spoke. There was no greeting, no hug, and no confrontation. We simply looked at one another, turned, and walked in opposite directions. The silence between us carried more weight than words could have.

That moment stayed with me long after the service ended. Linda had never been silent with me before. She always had something to say—encouragement, correction, advice, or simply a question about how I was doing. That evening, there was nothing, and the silence spoke loudly.

At the time, I told myself she simply needed time. Perhaps she needed space to process everything that had happened. Looking back, I think the silence affected me because somewhere deep inside I knew things were more complicated than I wanted to admit.

Still, Tameka and I continued moving forward. We were planning a wedding, building a future, and preparing for a life together. Like most couples standing at the edge of a new beginning, we believed we understood far more about ourselves than we actually did.

We could not yet see what would eventually be revealed or how deeply our covenant would be tested. We only knew that we loved one another and were moving toward marriage.

Chapter 2: Family Renewal Through Shared Ministry

Before Tameka and I ever stood together and made our vows, something else had to happen first. Our relationship had to find its place within our families.

Relationships do not exist in isolation. When two people come together, their lives are already connected to parents, siblings, children, friendships, histories, and expectations. Whether we recognize it or not, our choices ripple outward and touch the people who love us.

For a season, the tension surrounding my relationship with Tameka was not between Linda and Tameka. It was between Linda and me.

Linda loved me deeply, but she struggled with the path that had brought Tameka and me together. At that time, she did not really know Tameka personally. Her concern was about me, the choices I had made, and the direction my life had taken. Love sometimes shows itself through concern, and concern can create distance even when love has not disappeared. I understood that, even when it was difficult to carry.

When Linda finally met Tameka, I sensed a shift almost immediately. Their interaction had a warmth that gave me hope, though I was careful not to assume too much too quickly. Nothing was instantly resolved, but something had begun to soften.

What I did not recognize then was that GOD was laying a different kind of foundation.

My brother-in-law, Pastor Maynon Copeland, had a call to begin a ministry. Like many ministries that begin with more faith than resources, it did not start in a traditional church building. The first services were held outside at a school, and later the gatherings moved into their dining room. Chairs surrounded the table, Bibles were opened, prayers were offered, and week after week, people gathered faithfully. It was small and simple, but consistency slowly gave shape to something larger than any of us could see at the time.

As the ministry grew, it moved from the dining room into an office space in an office park. It was not the kind of place people usually imagine when they think of church, but what GOD was doing there was never dependent on appearance. Eventually, the congregation moved into a church building of its own, but the foundation had already been laid long before the building was purchased.

Somewhere along that journey, Tameka, the children, and I became part of it. At first, we were simply attending and learning the rhythms of this new church family. Over time, we became more involved and began serving alongside everyone else.

I began teaching Sunday School, and standing before a class with an open Bible became one of the ways my own life continued to be shaped. Preparing lessons required more than reading Scripture. It required me to consider whether what I was teaching was also being lived out.

From time to time, I was also asked to preach. Those opportunities carried weight for me, not because of the attention they brought, but because standing in that place made it harder to ignore what GOD still needed to address in me.

Tameka found her place in ministry as well. She helped with the children's choir, working patiently with young voices week after week, teaching worship songs, and encouraging the children as they stood before the congregation to sing. From the outside, that work may have looked simple, but it required patience, steadiness, and genuine care.

As time passed, people had the opportunity to know Tameka for themselves. They saw her serve, interact with others, and carry herself with consistency. Linda saw those things too. She was able to see more than the circumstances surrounding how our relationship began. She had the opportunity to really know Tameka and see the role she was playing in our family, our church, and our lives. What once felt uncertain became more familiar, and what once felt distant slowly moved closer.

Gradually, the distance between Linda and me began to ease. Conversations became more natural, and the tension that had shaped our interactions no longer weighed as heavily. It did not happen suddenly, but something was changing.

During that season, I thought we were simply attending church and serving where we were needed. Years later, I realized something deeper was taking place. While we were showing up week after week, relationships around us were being restored.

Before Tameka and I ever stood together and made our vows, the atmosphere surrounding our families had already begun to change. The tension that once existed was softening, trust was returning, and room was being made for what would come next.

Chapter 3: The Day We Made Our Vows

The day of our wedding did not feel like the beginning of our story. In many ways, it felt like the continuation of something that had already been developing over time. By the time we stood together and made our vows, our lives, our families, and even our faith had already begun to intertwine.

When we began preparing for the wedding, my divorce had been finalized. What had once been emotionally unsettled was now legally complete. I understood the seriousness of those decisions, especially as someone serving in ministry. That awareness was present even then, though I did not yet fully understand everything it required of me internally. The paperwork may have closed one chapter, but it did not erase the weight of how I had walked through it.

We did not enter that day pretending everything leading up to it had been simple. We came into it knowing that what had already happened could not be undone, and whatever future we built would require honesty, consistency, and a willingness to move forward together.

There was a quiet anticipation in the air as family and friends gathered. Weddings often carry mixed emotions, but for us, there was also gratitude. The road that brought us there had not been smooth, and some of the people standing with us understood that without needing it explained.

The man who officiated our wedding was Pastor Copeland, the same man who had opened his dining room for those early church gatherings. Standing beside him was Rev. Haynes, a mentor and true friend whose presence meant more to me than I expressed at the time. My sister Linda was there, and it mattered deeply to me that she and her husband were part of that moment. My oldest brother, William, stood with me as my best man, and my oldest daughter, Charity, stood beside Tameka as her maid of honor.

Rev. Haynes was the only minister and church leader from that earlier season of my life who attended the wedding. Others I invited were not there, including the one I had asked to stand with me. I understood their absence even then, and over time, I came to understand it more clearly. I did not hold it against them, but I did carry it quietly.

Our wedding reflected the season we were in. We held it at Tameka's mother's workplace, and Ms. Lottie prepared the food for the reception. It was not centered on presentation or formality. It was centered on the people who had walked with us and the relationships that had been given time to heal.

As the ceremony began, I felt calm yet deeply aware of the significance of what we were doing. It did not feel like a performance. It felt like a decision being made in front of people who had witnessed parts of the journey that led us there.

When we spoke our vows, they were simple and direct. We were not trying to present a perfect picture of ourselves. We were making a commitment, choosing to move forward together and trusting that what had begun in our lives would continue taking shape over time.

There is a moment during a wedding when everything changes quietly. Not because the room becomes silent, but because everyone present recognizes that something important is taking place. Standing there, I felt the weight of that moment not only in the words we were speaking, but in everything that had brought us to them.

After the ceremony, the day's structure gave way to conversation, laughter, and people reconnecting. Family members greeted each other, stories were shared, and the room settled into the kind of warmth that only develops when people have walked through difficult things together.

At one point during the reception, I watched Linda and Tameka embrace. It was not brief or distant. It was the kind of embrace that comes after tension has slowly given way to understanding. I had sensed signs of healing before then, but standing there watching them, I knew something had shifted.

I remember pulling out my camera and taking a picture of that moment. Even then, I knew I wanted to hold on to it. Over the years, I have taken thousands of photographs, but that image remains one of my most treasured possessions because it captured something much bigger than a hug.

Two of the most important women in my life were no longer standing on opposite sides of the past. They were standing together.

What I understand now is that what happened that day was about more than a ceremony. What filled that room had been forming long before we arrived at the altar. Relationships had already begun healing, hearts had already begun softening, and grace had already been at work among us.

At the time, I believed the wedding marked the beginning of our life together. Years later, I came to understand it meant more than just that. The vows were real, but they were not the completion of becoming one. They marked the beginning of a journey to be lived out through ordinary days, difficult seasons, growth, failure, forgiveness, and time.

The day we made our vows mattered deeply, but it was only part of the story. What we promised that day would eventually be tested, refined, and reshaped in ways neither of us yet understood.

Chapter 4: Blending Our Lives

After the wedding day passed and the celebrations quieted, what we had promised began to take shape in everyday life. A wedding lasts only a few hours, but the promise made there has to be lived out over the years. For Tameka and me, that meant learning to blend not only our lives, but also our families. Two adults, four children, two family histories, and two different ways of seeing the world were now sharing the same home.

Charity was eleven, Angelica was nine, Mayuni was eight, and Riakeye was six. Each of them brought a different personality, a different history, and a different set of expectations into the same space. What looked manageable in our minds required patience in real life.

We moved into a four-bedroom apartment to make room for everyone. Charity had her own room; Angelica and Mayuni shared a room; Riakeye had his own room; and Tameka and I had ours. The arrangement worked, but the real work was not where everyone slept. It was learning how to live together.

Those early days were filled with the details that make up family life. School mornings came early, and evenings were shaped by homework, dinner, and conversations about the day. Weekends had their own rhythm, with chores, errands, church activities, and time together as a family. Over time, those routines settled, and what once felt unfamiliar slowly became normal.

Church remained a steady part of our lives. The same place that had helped restore relationships within our family continued to shape the rhythm of our home. Week after week, we returned there to worship, serve, learn, and grow, often without realizing how deeply those routines were grounding us.

In those early years, we were learning how to build something together without fully understanding what still remained unfinished beneath the surface. Some things came together naturally. Others required patience as everyone adjusted to the new shape of our family.

Tameka had a natural way of creating warmth in the home. Through her interactions with the children and the routines she established, she helped create an environment where people felt cared for. Her presence shaped the atmosphere of our household in ways that were not always obvious in the moment, but became clearer with time.

Our different upbringings quietly influenced how we approached parenting. Tameka grew up in a home where conversation played a central role. Her mother, Ms. Lottie, talked with her, explained things, and created connection through communication. My upbringing carried a different rhythm. My mother, Ms. Alice, taught mostly through example. There were not many long conversations about how to do things. I learned by watching her—how she carried herself, how she worked, and how she maintained order in our home. Those lessons stayed with me and shaped the way I approached parenting.

Both of us also understood what it meant to grow up in homes where our fathers were not consistently present. I can clearly remember only one season when my father, Mr. Earlie, lived in the home with us during my childhood. What remains most vivid from that time was an argument between him and my mother. I could say more about that day, but what matters most is that it was the last time the three of us lived together under the same roof. Tameka remembered earlier years with both of her parents before her father eventually left the household as well.

Even so, our fathers remained part of our lives. We spent time with them, and over time, we were introduced to stepmothers, step-siblings, and expanding family dynamics that reshaped what family looked like for both of us.

Those experiences influenced how we viewed parenting and relationships. Tameka's father, Mr. Henry, enjoys conversation and always has a story or joke ready to share. My father is quieter by nature, though we talk far more now than we did when I was younger. My stepmother, Ms. Diane, became someone I could confide in, filling a space I did not fully recognize at the time.

Because of those different backgrounds, our parenting styles reflected the homes we came from. Tameka connected with the children through conversation, helping them process thoughts and emotions, while I tended to be more direct. I gave instructions and expected things to be done a certain way, even as I tried to approach that responsibility with care.

As the years passed, I found myself wondering how our children experienced those differences. One day, they will tell their own stories about what it felt like growing up in that environment. What I do know is that both of us were trying to provide stability, guidance, structure, and love in the best way we knew how.

Many of the most meaningful moments during that season were ordinary ones. Sitting around the dinner table, driving to activities, helping with homework, or listening to conversations during car rides became part of the quiet work that was drawing us together. At the time, those moments seemed small, but they slowly became part of the foundation we were building.

Like any household, we faced challenges. There were disagreements to work through, schedules to manage, bills to pay, and the constant effort of making sure everyone's needs were being met. Gradually, our apartment became more than a place where we lived. It began to feel like home.

Blending our lives also meant blending our extended families. From the beginning, Tameka's family did not treat me like someone who had simply married into the family. They welcomed me as though I already belonged there. Her father, mother, brother, and the many uncles, aunties, and cousins on both sides of the family embraced me in a way that made the transition feel natural.

Over the years, we attended family reunions, birthday celebrations, funerals, and holiday gatherings together. Somewhere along the way, I realized I was no longer attending those events as a guest. I had become part of the family.

Tameka's father and I developed our own rhythm over time. He would call to talk about sports, share a joke, or simply check in, and those conversations reflected the ease that had formed between us.

Something similar was happening within my own family. Tameka developed a close relationship with my stepmother, Ms. Diane. Whenever we visited my father's house, the same pattern often unfolded. Tameka and my stepmother would talk in the kitchen or dining room while my father and I settled into another room to watch sports. It was a simple scene, but it reflected how naturally she had become woven into my family. She also attended ministers' wives' meetings alongside my sister Linda, and over time, their relationship grew closer.

Many of my favorite memories from that season center around the children. One tradition I especially enjoyed was attending May Day events at their elementary schools. Because my schedule was more flexible, I was often the parent able to attend during the school day. Those events were filled with laughter and activity—three-legged races, sack races, water balloon tosses, and tug-of-war games. I still remember watching the children glance towards the crowd, searching for familiar faces, and feeling an overwhelming sense of gratitude simply for being present.

Experiences like those may seem small while they are happening, but they gradually become woven into the fabric of family life. Each one quietly strengthened the bonds forming within our home.

For a season, everything appeared to settle into a steady rhythm. Our home was forming, the children were growing, and the routines of everyday life began to feel dependable. From the outside, everything seemed to be moving in the right direction, and in many ways it was.

Years later, I realized that even during seasons that feel steady, there are often things beneath the surface that remain unseen. As parents, we notice much, but we do not see everything. There were parts of our children's experiences we did not fully understand at the time. Some things became clearer later, and some things may never be fully known.

That realization has stayed with me. It reminds me that building something with care does not always mean we fully understand everything unfolding within it.

During that season, we were simply living our lives—raising children, building a home, serving in church, and moving forward with a sense of stability that felt dependable. It was easy to believe that what we were building would continue in the same direction.

What I understand now is that blending lives is only the beginning. The deeper work often takes place beneath the surface, in places that are not immediately visible. At the time, we were not thinking about that. We were simply living, trusting that what we were building would continue to hold.

For a while, it seemed like it would.

PART II — WHEN LOVE TOLD THE TRUTH

Love does not eliminate the need for truth. Over time, what had remained hidden beneath the surface began to reveal itself in ordinary life until it could no longer be ignored.

What followed was more than the exposure of actions. It revealed patterns, assumptions, and struggles that had been shaping choices for years. Facing those realities was painful, but it became the beginning of a deeper honesty than either of us had known before. What follows traces that journey into the light and the truths that demanded to be confronted before anything could truly change.

Chapter 5: When Everything Came Into the Light

It began on what seemed like an ordinary Saturday morning. There had been no argument the night before, no lingering tension, and nothing unresolved to suggest something was wrong. Our marriage felt steady. We were affectionate, connected, and moving through life with the quiet rhythm of two people building something meaningful together. Nothing about that morning suggested it would become a turning point in our story.

When my body did not respond the way it always had, confusion surfaced first, followed by embarrassment and then a quiet but unmistakable panic. Desire had always produced response, and somewhere along the way, I had attached part of my confidence to that reliability without realizing how deeply. In that moment, what seemed physical exposed something much deeper within me.

I had tied part of my identity, even my sense of masculinity, to performance. I would not have admitted that out loud at the time, but sitting there in the silence of that room, I felt the weight of it.

Tameka responded gently, without accusation or visible frustration. She offered reassurance and concern, but even while she was trying to comfort me, I had already started retreating inward. My thoughts began racing toward explanations that would help me regain control. I thought about stress, exhaustion, possible medical problems, anything that could give me a technical answer for what was beginning to feel like a deeper vulnerability.

The moment itself passed, but my mind never really left it. I replayed it repeatedly, quietly measuring myself against what had happened. Awareness slowly became monitoring, and monitoring eventually became testing. Underneath all of it was fear I did not yet know how to name.

As time passed, that pressure began affecting me physically again. It is difficult to respond with confidence when your thoughts are filled with doubt. What I had tried to dismiss as an isolated moment was beginning to feel like something larger than I could simply manage away.

At the same time, my lifestyle had quietly changed. I spent most of my free time sitting on the couch watching sports, rarely exercising, and paying little attention to what that lack of discipline was doing to my body. In trying to understand what was happening physically, I was also being forced to confront areas of my life I had neglected emotionally and spiritually.

Over the following weeks and months, I carried that insecurity quietly. Outwardly, little appeared different. I continued teaching, preaching, working, leading, and showing up at home, and our routines remained intact. Internally, however, something in me was becoming unsettled. I convinced myself the issue was temporary and that I could resolve it without drawing attention to it.

I did not invite conversation or confess vulnerability. Instead, I relied on self-management, believing I could handle everything privately. Looking back now, I can see how much of my life had become organized around maintaining appearances rather than honestly understanding what was happening within me. I mistook control for health, but control without honesty only delays exposure.

I still did not fully understand what I was dealing with. I thought the problem was mainly stress and insecurity, but something deeper was happening beneath the surface. Before my salvation and before answering the call to ministry, pornography and masturbation had been part of my life. When I gave my life to CHRIST and surrendered to His call, those struggles disappeared. For years, they simply were not part of my life, and I believed that chapter had been permanently closed.

Because of that, I never considered them a future danger. I assumed the victory GOD had given me in those areas meant the battle itself was over. Looking back, I realize I misunderstood something important. The behavior had disappeared, but I had never fully examined the underlying issues. I had not yet learned how insecurity, the desire for affirmation, fear, and vulnerability could create openings in places I thought were already settled.

The relationship Tameka and I entered before my divorce was final should have been a warning to me, but I did not see it that way at the time. I focused on the sincerity of our feelings for one another and ignored the fact that I was already letting my emotions overrule what I knew was right. I did not realize that a compromise in one area of life can weaken a person's resistance in other areas. Something within me had already begun shifting long before that Saturday morning, even though I could not see it clearly.

When insecurity entered the picture after that morning, old ways of thinking resurfaced. What I had once left behind began returning. Pornography and masturbation reappeared, not because they had secretly remained part of my life all those years, but because I was turning to familiar forms of escape instead of honestly confronting what was happening within me.

At first, I viewed those behaviors as separate from the larger struggles developing in my life. I thought I was dealing with a physical problem, an emotional problem, or a marital problem. I did not yet understand how connected everything was. What I could not see was that the same desire for comfort, affirmation, escape, and control was shaping it all.

What I had tried to contain in my thoughts eventually began to shape my actions. The boundaries I believed I was managing were crossed, and what began as a hidden struggle moved beyond pornography and self-gratification into an involvement with another woman. Even then, I convinced myself I could end it quietly and fix everything without anyone knowing how far things had gone.

That illusion did not last.

The truth surfaced in the most unexpected way during family prayer, when I said that woman's name instead of my wife's. There were no raised voices and no immediate confrontation, only a heavy silence that made it clear what I had tried to keep hidden was now visible.

What followed was confusion, distance, and disorientation. I said I needed space to think, but in reality, I was still trying to maintain control over something that was already collapsing. For a short season, our family lived apart, not because clarity had come, but because I was wavering. I was still trying to preserve pieces of a divided life that could no longer remain divided.

Living that way required constant effort. I was monitoring my words, managing appearances, anticipating exposure, and maintaining different versions of myself depending on where I was and who I was with. It was exhausting, even when it looked controlled from the outside. What I called management was actually fragmentation.

When my mother discovered what had happened, she responded out of concern and reached out for help. She asked my oldest brother, William, to speak with me, not out of judgment, but out of love. At the same time, my brother-in-law, Pastor Copeland, and my oldest sister,

Linda, began praying quietly and bringing the situation before GOD. Years later, I came to understand more fully how much those prayers mattered, even though I could not fully recognize it then.

While Tameka and I were trying to process everything, the children were living inside it. Children understand more than we often realize, and even when we try to shield them, they can sense when something has shifted. One moment from that season has stayed with me over the years. My stepson, Riakeye, the youngest, looked at me and asked, "Did you cheat on Mom?"

That question removed any distance I had tried to place between my actions and their impact. What I had done was no longer something I could frame, minimize, or manage privately. It had reached the entire family.

A couple of years later, while watching the film The Family That Preys, one line settled on me in a way I could not ignore: "You can't make yourself happy, bringing misery to other people." Even then, I did not fully understand everything happening within me, but I could no longer deny the weight of what I had done.

Over time, I came to understand something I could not fully see during that season. I had spent years believing I could separate parts of my life, allowing some things to remain visible while keeping others hidden. I thought ministry, responsibility, and outward stability could compensate for what I refused to confront privately. But what remains hidden never truly stays contained. Eventually, it finds its way into the open, often in ways we would never choose for ourselves.

When everything came into the light, it did not feel like relief. It felt like exposure. It brought an end to the version of control I thought I had, and there was no returning to the life I had tried to manage privately.

At the time, exposure felt like destruction. What I understand now is that it was a revelation, too. What came into the light was painful, humiliating, and costly, but it uncovered what had been quietly forming within me for most of my life. What I had mistaken for strength was often self-management. What I had mistaken for control was often concealment. And what I had mistaken for spiritual maturity was, in some places, still unfinished surrender.

The truth did not merely expose what I had done. It exposed what had been happening within me long before I was willing to name it.

Chapter 6: The Problem Beneath the Problem

When everything came into the light, it was easy to focus on the affair because it was the most visible part of the story. It was the event everyone could see, the decision that created immediate damage, and the thing that forced long-hidden issues into the open. Yet as I spent more time examining that season of my life, I began to realize the affair itself was not the beginning of the problem. What became visible through my actions had been forming within me for much longer than I understood at the time.

During those years, I believed the struggles I had experienced before my salvation were behind me. Before coming to CHRIST, pornography and masturbation had been part of my life, but when I surrendered my life to GOD and answered the call to ministry, those things disappeared. I did not spend years secretly fighting those behaviors while preaching and serving. They were simply gone, and because they were gone, I assumed the underlying issues had been dealt with as well.

That assumption shaped how I viewed myself for many years. I believed I had experienced complete victory in those areas, and in many ways I had. I was focused on ministry, committed to my family, and satisfied within my marriage. The life Tameka and I were building felt healthy and stable. We were raising children, serving in church, maintaining a home, and moving through the normal responsibilities of life together. Looking back, I can honestly say that many parts of that season were good.

What I failed to recognize was that the absence of a behavior does not necessarily mean that every issue associated with it has been addressed. I never stopped to ask what had existed beneath those earlier struggles because I no longer felt any need to. As long as life felt stable, there seemed to be no reason to examine those deeper places within myself. Because my life was functioning well, I assumed everything within me was healthy. Because I was serving effectively, I assumed I was surrendering completely. Because I was avoiding certain behaviors, I assumed I had fully overcome the vulnerabilities that once contributed to them.

The longer life remained steady, the more confident I became in those assumptions. When I look back now, I can see how much trust I placed in my ability to manage myself. I believed discipline, responsibility, and good intentions would be enough to keep me on the right path. If I continued doing the things I was supposed to do, I assumed the deeper issues would take care of themselves. Much of my confidence rested in my ability to maintain control, but I eventually learned that control and surrender are not the same thing.

As time passed, I also failed to recognize how thoughts shape direction. Most destructive choices do not appear suddenly. They begin much earlier in ways that seem insignificant. A thought is entertained rather than challenged. A feeling is justified rather than examined. A boundary becomes easier to move because it no longer feels necessary. What appears small at first gradually gains influence when left unaddressed. Long before a decision becomes visible, something has usually been developing beneath the surface.

When I think about the relationship Tameka and I entered before my divorce was final, I can see evidence of that pattern at work. Although pornography and masturbation were not part of my life during that period, my thinking had already begun changing. I allowed emotions to guide decisions that should have been governed by conviction. I justified what I wanted because I believed the outcome was already inevitable. Instead of submitting my desires to what I knew was right, I convinced myself that my feelings somehow justified my actions.

At the time, I did not see that as part of a larger problem. I viewed it as a unique situation connected to specific circumstances. Years later, I understand it differently. The behavior looked different, but some of the underlying issues were remarkably similar. I was still relying on my own reasoning. I was still trusting my own judgment. I was still finding ways to justify what I wanted rather than honestly confronting what was happening within me.

Those patterns remained largely unnoticed because life continued moving forward. I was preaching, teaching, serving, working, and fulfilling responsibilities. From the outside, there was little reason for anyone to believe something deeper was taking shape beneath the surface. The truth is, I did not recognize it either. Serving in ministry added another layer to that reality because the more visible my role became, the more difficult it felt to admit weakness. Instead of bringing the struggles to light while they were still small, I convinced myself I could handle them privately. I believed that if I could simply regain control, there would be no reason for anyone else to know what was happening.

That way of thinking seemed reasonable at the time, but it was slowly creating problems of its own. I became more concerned with preserving the appearance of stability than understanding why stability was becoming harder to maintain. Ministry responsibilities, church involvement, and outward productivity enabled me to avoid questions I should have been asking myself. None of this means my faith was insincere. I genuinely loved GOD. I believed His Word, taught His Word, and wanted to live faithfully. Yet loving GOD and fully surrendering every area of life are not always the same thing. There were still places within me that had never been examined honestly enough to be healed completely.

When pornography and masturbation returned after that Saturday morning, and by the time the affair developed, the conditions that allowed those choices were already present. The crisis did not create those deeper issues. It exposed them. What became visible through my actions revealed patterns, vulnerabilities, and ways of thinking that had been operating unnoticed for years. The affair was not the beginning of the story. It was the point where the story could no longer remain hidden.

Understanding that there was a problem beneath the problem did not automatically change me. Insight and action are not the same thing. I was beginning to see things I had not seen before, but seeing them and responding to them were two different matters.

During that season, Tameka's mother, Ms. Lottie, spoke to me in a way that I have never forgotten. She had always treated me with kindness and respect. Even after everything that had happened, she never approached me with hostility or condemnation. She loved her daughter deeply, but she also cared about me.

During one conversation, she told me that Tameka was approaching her breaking point and that if things continued the way they were, I was going to lose her. Those words stayed with me long after the conversation ended because they forced me to look beyond my own confusion, guilt, and fear. Until then, much of my attention had been focused on what I was experiencing. Ms. Lottie helped me see what everyone else was experiencing. The person being hurt most by my choices was the woman I claimed to love. My children were being affected. Our family was being affected. The people who cared about us were being affected. What I had spent so much time viewing through the lens of my own struggle suddenly appeared from a completely different perspective.

Looking back, I do not see that conversation as the beginning of recovery. I see it as the moment I stopped believing that small adjustments would be enough. It forced me to recognize that if my marriage was going to survive, real change would be required. For the first time, I truly understood what was at stake, and that realization became the beginning of something different.

Chapter 7: The Cost and the Gift of Staying

When the truth came into the light, Tameka faced a decision she never expected to make. She could walk away from the damage that had been done, or she could remain and face it with me. Neither choice was easy, and neither came without pain. Looking back, I have come to appreciate that the decision itself was only the beginning. Choosing to stay did not remove the hurt, restore trust, or answer the questions that remained between us. It simply created the possibility that those things might eventually happen.

Once we both chose to remain in the marriage, the focus of our lives changed. The crisis had already forced us to confront what could no longer be ignored, but the days that followed revealed a different challenge. The question was no longer whether our marriage would survive. The question became how we would live within the reality of what had happened. Whatever our relationship became after that season would be shaped less by emotional promises and more by the ordinary choices we made every day afterward.

At first, everything felt uncertain. We continued to share a home, share responsibilities, and move through the routines of family life, but nothing felt quite the same. Trust had been damaged, and neither of us knew how long it would take to rebuild. Some days felt hopeful. Other days felt fragile. There was no clear roadmap for moving forward, and there were moments when even small conversations carried a weight they never would have carried before. We were learning that healing is rarely dramatic. More often, it unfolds slowly through decisions that seem ordinary as they happen.

One of the hardest lessons for me involved surrendering control over the pace of trust. Earlier in life, I believed that sincere apologies, honest conversations, and visible effort would naturally produce restoration. What I eventually learned was that trust does not return according to the timetable of the person who damaged it. Tameka had every reason to be cautious. There were times when I answered questions honestly and still sensed hesitation in her response. There were moments when I wanted reassurance that things were improving and evidence that my efforts were making a difference. Over time, however, I came to understand that her caution was not rejection. It was wisdom shaped by experience.

That realization forced me to shift my focus. Instead of asking whether trust was returning, I had to ask whether I was becoming trustworthy. My responsibility was not to determine when Tameka should feel safe again. My responsibility was to live honestly, consistently, and transparently, regardless of whether I saw immediate results. Trust grows through repeated experiences, and repeated experiences require time. There was no shortcut around that reality.

One of the practical changes that emerged during that season was complete transparency. Tameka had access to my phone, my computer, every area of my digital life, and anything else she needed. Earlier in my life, I might have viewed that as an invasion of privacy or a restriction on my independence. After everything that had happened, I saw it differently. Secrecy had played a role in damaging our marriage, and openness became part of rebuilding it. Transparency was not punishment. It was one of the ways

I learned to stop dividing my life into separate compartments and begin living with greater integrity.

What surprised me most was how often trust was rebuilt through ordinary moments rather than dramatic ones. It was rebuilt when I followed through on commitments. It was rebuilt when I answered difficult questions without becoming defensive. It was rebuilt when I was where I said I would be and did what I said I would do. None of those moments felt particularly significant on their own, yet together they began to create a pattern of consistency that had not existed before. Over time, those ordinary moments carried more weight than any speech or promise ever could.

While I was learning those lessons, Tameka was carrying a burden I could not fully understand. She had to decide how she would live with what she now knew. The betrayal could have surfaced in every disagreement, every disappointment, and every difficult conversation. There were moments when old wounds naturally resurfaced and moments when she had every reason to revisit what had happened. Yet over time, I watched her make a choice that required a strength I did not fully appreciate at the time.

She refused to allow the worst chapter of our marriage to become the only chapter of our marriage.

That did not mean she ignored the pain or pretended it never happened. It did not mean she excused my choices or forgot what they had cost. It meant she was learning to hold the truth without allowing it to define every interaction that followed. Looking back, I can see how difficult that must have been. Remaining emotionally present after trust has been broken requires a kind of courage that is often invisible to everyone except the person carrying it.

One memory from that season has remained with me over the years. Throughout our marriage, I was always the one taking photographs. Birthdays, holidays, vacations, family gatherings, and ordinary moments all found their way into albums filled with memories. When I look back at that particular year, however, the photographs tell a different story. There are only fourteen pictures from the entire year, and only one of them includes Tameka.

The picture was taken at a museum. She appears composed and calm, yet there is a distance in her expression that I still notice whenever I look at it. For a long time, I avoided that photograph because it forced me to sit with what my choices had cost. Eventually, I began seeing it differently. The picture reminds me that healing was not immediate and that rebuilding trust demanded far more than good intentions. It reminds me that simply remaining together during that season required strength from both of us.

As time passed, something between us slowly began to change. The change was not dramatic enough to announce itself, and neither of us could point to a single conversation that fixed everything. Instead, healing revealed itself gradually. Conversations became less guarded. Questions felt less threatening. Tension no longer lingered as long as it once had. We became more willing to address concerns before they grew into larger problems. Without fully realizing it, we were developing habits that made honesty easier and avoidance more difficult.

One of the most important changes involved learning how to remain in uncomfortable conversations. Earlier in our relationship, we often postponed discussions because they felt difficult. During this season, we learned to stay with those conversations longer. We learned how to listen more carefully, ask better questions, and resist the urge to become defensive. We learned that understanding one another often required patience rather than immediate solutions. Those lessons were not learned all at once, but they gradually changed the atmosphere of our marriage.

The longer we remained committed to that process, the more we discovered that staying together was doing more than preserving a marriage. It was changing us. I was learning humility because I could no longer control how quickly trust returned. Tameka demonstrated courage by remaining emotionally present after being hurt, a feat that required tremendous strength. Both of us were learning patience because neither healing nor trust could be rushed.

The fracture never disappeared completely from our story. Certain memories remain, and some consequences cannot be undone. Yet over time, the fracture stopped controlling the marriage. It stopped defining every conversation and shaping every interaction. What once occupied so much space between us gradually lost its influence as trust began growing in its place.

We did not heal by pretending the past had never happened, nor by remaining trapped within it. We moved forward by remaining present with one another, especially during moments when distance would have been easier.

Day after day, often in ways that seemed small at the time, we practiced staying.

As the years passed, I came to understand that staying had given us something as well as costing us something. It cost us certainty. It cost us the ability to move through marriage, assuming trust would always be there without being protected and nurtured. It cost us a season of innocence that we could never fully recover. We both carried memories that could not simply be erased, and rebuilding required emotional energy, difficult conversations, accountability, patience, and time.

Yet staying also gave us something. It gave us the opportunity to build a marriage that rested less on appearances and more on truth. It gave us the opportunity to know one another more honestly than we had before. It gave us the opportunity to discover that grace is not only what helps a marriage survive a crisis. Grace is what teaches two imperfect people how to remain present with one another long after the crisis has passed.

By the time we began recognizing a new steadiness in our marriage, we understood something we had not fully understood before. Staying was never a single decision made in a moment of emotion. It was a commitment practiced repeatedly over time. Through that practice, something new was being built between us. We did not yet realize how much deeper that work would eventually go, but the foundation was being laid for the next stage of our journey—one that would help us understand not only what had happened, but why it had happened and how GOD would use that understanding to continue transforming both of us.

PART III — WHEN GRACE BUILT A HOME

Exposure was not the end of the story. What came into the light revealed what needed to change, but change itself required more than regret or good intentions.

The work that followed unfolded through recovery, accountability, honesty, humility, and a growing dependence on GOD. What emerged was not a return to the marriage we once had, but the gradual formation of something stronger—built on truth, shaped by grace, and sustained by a deeper understanding of one another. What grace built was not perfection but a home where two imperfect people could continue to become one.

Chapter 8: The Work Grace Did Within Us

By the time recovery entered our lives, some important things had already begun to change. The affair had ended. Tameka and I had chosen to remain together. Trust was slowly being rebuilt, and our marriage was beginning to find a measure of stability again. The constant uncertainty that had defined the earliest days after everything came into the light was beginning to ease. We were no longer asking whether our marriage would survive. We were trying to learn how to live within the reality of what had happened and build something healthier than what had existed before. Those changes were real, and they mattered, but as grateful as I was for the progress we were making, I knew something deeper still needed to be addressed. The marriage was beginning to heal, yet I still could not fully explain why I had made the choices I had made or why determination alone had failed to produce lasting change.

For most of my life, I believed that if I wanted something badly enough, I could discipline myself into becoming it. That approach had worked in many areas of my life. It had helped me succeed in the military, advance in my career, and fulfill responsibilities in ministry. Whenever I encountered a problem, my instinct was to work harder, become more disciplined, and push through it. What I was beginning to discover, however, was that some struggles do not respond to effort alone. The more honestly I examined my life, the more I realized that I had spent years addressing symptoms while avoiding deeper questions. I could clearly identify the visible failures that had damaged my marriage, but I still did not understand the patterns that had produced them. The affair had not appeared out of nowhere. It had grown out of ways of thinking, coping, and seeking affirmation that had been developing for years, and until I understood those things, I knew I was only addressing part of the problem.

That realization sent me searching for answers. I began reading, researching, and trying to understand whether there were resources that could help me make sense of what I was experiencing. During that search, I came across information about Sexaholics Anonymous. My initial reaction was skepticism. I did not see myself in the image I had created of what addiction looked like. I was still employed. I was still preaching and teaching. I was still paying bills, caring for my family, and carrying responsibilities. In my mind, addiction belonged to people whose lives had completely unraveled. Yet the more I read, the more difficult it became to dismiss what I was finding. The descriptions focused less on outward consequences and more on the internal patterns behind them. They described secrecy, compartmentalization, rationalization, and the exhausting effort required to maintain different versions of yourself depending on where you were and who you were with. As I read those descriptions, I began recognizing pieces of myself in ways that made me increasingly uncomfortable.

Eventually, I decided to attend a meeting. Walking into that room felt unfamiliar and humbling. I was not entirely sure I belonged there, and part of me expected to leave convinced that whatever was wrong with me had a different explanation. Instead, I sat and listened. As men shared their stories, I heard experiences that sounded remarkably familiar. The circumstances were not always identical, but the underlying themes kept repeating themselves. Men talked about living divided lives, chasing affirmation, hiding weakness, managing appearances, and convincing themselves they remained in control long after control had begun slipping away. The longer I listened, the less interested I became in comparing details and the more focused I became on the similarities. For the first time, I began to consider the possibility that what I was facing was more than a collection of bad decisions. The decisions mattered, and I was responsible for every one of them, but they were connected to deeper patterns that I had never honestly confronted.

As recovery became part of my life, it gave language to things I had never fully understood. It helped me recognize that many of the struggles I thought were separate were actually connected. The need for affirmation, the tendency to manage appearances, the habit of hiding weakness, and the belief that I could solve everything privately were not isolated issues. They reinforced one another in ways I had never recognized. What had happened in my marriage did not begin with an affair. The affair was the most visible expression of patterns that had been shaping my thinking and behavior for years. Some of those patterns stretched back long before I met Tameka. Others had become so familiar that I no longer questioned them. Recovery forced me to stop looking only at the damage and begin examining the roots beneath it. The more I understood those deeper patterns, the more I realized they affected far more than the decisions that had brought me into recovery. They had shaped the way I viewed myself, related to others, handled disappointment, sought affirmation, and even understood my relationship with GOD.

What surprised me most was that recovery affected far more than my behavior. It challenged the way I understood strength, responsibility, honesty, and even my relationship with GOD. For years, I had approached life believing that self-sufficiency was a virtue. If something was broken, I assumed I could fix it. If something was wrong, I assumed I could overcome it with discipline and determination. Recovery exposed the limits of that thinking. It revealed how often I had relied on effort while avoiding vulnerability and how frequently I had mistaken self-management for genuine transformation. The more I learned, the more I realized that dependence on GOD is not the opposite of strength. In many ways, it is where true strength begins. What I could not accomplish through willpower alone, GOD began addressing through honesty, accountability, surrender, and grace.

Recovery also became part of our marriage. This was not something happening only to me while Tameka observed from a distance. She attended meetings with me, learned alongside me, and became part of a process that was changing both of us in ways neither of us fully expected. We were both learning, both growing, and both being challenged to examine ourselves honestly. One of the most significant lessons we learned during that season was that neither of us was perfect, and neither of us could build a healthy marriage by focusing exclusively on the other person's shortcomings. I am careful when discussing this because parts of that story belong to Tameka and are hers to tell, but I can say that recovery created space for both of us to take responsibility for ourselves in ways we had not before. It encouraged us to spend less time defending ourselves and more time listening. It challenged us to move beyond assigning blame and begin understanding the fears, expectations, disappointments, and assumptions that shaped how we related to one another.

Those changes began affecting the way we communicated. Conversations became deeper because they were no longer focused solely on behavior. We began talking about why we responded the way we did, what we feared, what we expected from one another, and how our individual histories influenced our reactions. We learned that many disagreements were not really about the immediate issue being discussed. They were often connected to something deeper that neither of us had fully recognized. As we became more aware of those dynamics, we also became more patient with one another. I learned to give Tameka space when she needed time to process her thoughts, and she learned that difficult conversations did not have to become destructive. Those changes did not happen overnight, but they gradually created a safer environment for honesty and understanding.

I believe recovery taught us something we had not fully understood before. Love is sustained not only by affection, attraction, or commitment, but by truth. The more honestly we learned to live, the more honestly we learned to love. That did not mean every problem disappeared or that every disagreement suddenly became easy. We still misunderstood one another at times. We still carried habits that needed attention. We still had moments when patience was required. The difference was that we were approaching those moments differently. We were becoming less concerned with defending ourselves and more concerned with understanding one another. We were learning to move toward one another rather than away from one another.

What grace was doing during that season went far beyond repairing the damage I had caused. It was reshaping the foundation of our marriage. It was teaching us humility where we once relied on certainty, honesty where we once relied on appearances, and dependence on GOD where we once relied primarily on ourselves. The work was rarely dramatic, and most of it unfolded in ordinary conversations, daily choices, and small acts of faithfulness. Yet over time, those ordinary moments produced extraordinary results. The marriage that emerged from that season was not built on the assumption that we had finally figured everything out. It was built on a growing willingness to remain honest, take responsibility, seek help when needed, and continue growing together.

The work grace did within us was not completed in a meeting, a conversation, or a single breakthrough. It unfolded gradually over the years, and in many ways it continues even now. What changed was not simply our behavior but our willingness to live truthfully before GOD and one another. Recovery gave us tools, language, and understanding, but grace gave those things life. Together, they helped transform a season that could have marked the end of our story into the beginning of a different one. We were no longer simply rebuilding trust. We were learning new ways of relating to one another, new ways of understanding ourselves, and new ways of expressing love. The lessons we learned during that season continue to shape how we live, love, and become one today.

Chapter 9: Learning a Different Kind of Love

One of the most important things I learned during those years was that understanding another person requires more than simply living with them. By the time recovery had become part of our lives, Tameka and I had already spent years together. We had raised children, shared responsibilities, built routines, and walked through seasons of joy and hardship. Yet I was beginning to realize there were still parts of her I did not fully understand.

One of those areas involved the way she processes her thoughts and feelings. Tameka has always been someone who takes time to think through things before speaking. During the earlier years of our marriage, I often struggled with that. When she became quiet, I immediately assumed something was wrong. My mind would begin searching for an explanation, and I often pushed for a conversation before she was ready. Because she was still processing, she could not always explain exactly what she was feeling, and because I wanted answers immediately, I often responded to things she had not fully said.

The result was frustration for both of us. Looking back, I can see that her silence was never really the problem. The problem was my discomfort with uncertainty. I wanted immediate answers because uncertainty made me anxious. I wanted resolution because I believed unresolved things were dangerous. Over time, however, I began to understand that not every silence needs to be filled and not every conversation needs to happen immediately. Learning to give Tameka space required me to become more patient than I had been before. It also required me to trust that when she was ready to talk, she would. The more I respected that process, the healthier our conversations became. She felt less pressure, and I became a better listener. Instead of trying to force understanding, I learned to wait for it.

That lesson affected far more than a single area of our marriage. It changed the way we approached conflict as well. Earlier in our relationship, difficult conversations often felt like problems that needed to be solved as quickly as possible. If tension appeared, both of us wanted it resolved. Over time, however, we learned that understanding is not always immediate. Some issues required discussion, reflection, prayer, and time. We stopped viewing every disagreement as something that threatened the relationship and began treating disagreements as opportunities to understand one another more fully. We became more willing to remain present with one another while understanding developed, trusting that a conversation did not have to be finished in a single sitting to be productive.

As those changes accumulated over time, we began noticing something neither of us could have forced. The marriage was becoming less defined by what had happened and more defined by what we were becoming. Trust was no longer the only thing growing between us. Friendship, understanding, affection, and emotional safety were also growing. We found ourselves talking more openly, laughing more freely, and sharing thoughts that might once have remained private. Questions felt safer. Defensiveness appeared less often. The relationship gradually became a place where honesty felt more natural than hiding.

We also became truly intimate again, not as an attempt to erase the past, but as another sign that trust, affection, and closeness were returning to our marriage. What was developing between us felt different from what we had known before. Earlier in our marriage, much of our closeness had been built on love, attraction, shared responsibilities, and the excitement of building a life together. What was emerging now carried a different depth. It had been tested by disappointment, strengthened through honesty, and shaped by experiences neither of us would have chosen.

One evening during that season, Tameka said something simple that carried more meaning than either of us would have expected years earlier.

"I love you more."

Tameka had told me she loved me before, but adding the word "more" carried a different weight. The phrase no longer reflected only affection. It carried the weight of everything we had walked through together. It carried memories of difficult conversations, painful truths, patient rebuilding, and the decision to remain committed even when remaining had been difficult. When I answered, "I love you more than more," it felt less like a playful exchange and more like the language of two people who understood something they had not understood before.

Those words were no longer simply about how we felt. They reflected what we had experienced together and what we had learned through those experiences.

Years later, she gave me a framed picture with the words "Love You More" printed across it. She did not make a speech when she handed it to me. She simply gave it to me, and it has hung above my dresser ever since. Every morning and every night, I see those words. They remind me not only of affection, but of growth. They remind me of a season when both of us were being changed. They remind me of conversations that stretched us, truths that humbled us, and lessons that neither of us would have chosen but both of us needed.

Most of all, they remind me that love became something deeper than what either of us understood at the beginning of our marriage.

Learning a different kind of love did not mean returning to who we had been before. The people we were before could not have built the marriage we have now. What emerged from that season was not a restoration of the old relationship, but the creation of something different. We learned to be more honest, more patient, and more willing to take responsibility for ourselves. We discovered that love grows deeper when it is shaped by truth rather than protected by appearances.

The relationship was no longer defined primarily by what had happened years earlier. The past remained part of our story, but it no longer occupied its center. What stood in its place was something far more valuable: a deeper understanding of one another, a greater dependence on GOD, and a love strengthened through honesty, responsibility, growth, and grace.

At the time, neither of us realized how important those lessons would become. The years of rebuilding had taught us how to remain with one another through pain, disappointment, and uncertainty. Before long, life would place us in a different kind of season, one that had nothing to do with recovery and everything to do with loss. What we had learned through the past years would soon help us carry one another through grief in ways we could not yet see.

Chapter 10: Two Calls, Two Rides, One GOD at Work

The phone rang the way it always had, yet something about that moment felt different. Some calls bring ordinary news. Others quietly divide life into before and after. Tameka answered, and I watched her expression change before I heard a single word. Her brother's voice carried a weight that required no explanation. Her mother, Ms. Lottie, was gone.

We dressed quietly and began the drive to the senior living complex where she lived. The car was filled with a silence that felt heavier than the road itself. Tameka sat beside me, not overcome with emotion, but absorbing the moment in the steady way she often did. I gripped the steering wheel tighter than necessary, not because of traffic, but because steadiness felt necessary. Whatever I was feeling could wait. In that moment, my role was clear. She needed anchoring, and I understood that without either of us saying it aloud.

Only a few days earlier, her mother had been sitting in that same car with us. We had driven her back to the complex and pulled up near the entrance. I stepped out and walked around to help her, asking whether she needed assistance getting inside or up to her apartment, but she declined as she often did, carrying that familiar blend of independence and quiet humor. We watched her walk through the doors and toward the elevator, fully expecting we would see her again soon. Nothing about that moment suggested it would be the last time.

Grief does not always give you time to prepare. When it comes suddenly, it interrupts everything. It changes the atmosphere of a home without moving a single object. Conversations become shorter, silence becomes longer, and responsibilities keep pressing forward while emotions are still trying to catch up. Life continues moving, but something central has stopped.

In the days that followed, responsibility settled on us in a quiet but unavoidable way. We handled arrangements, made phone calls, finalized decisions, and coordinated details while grief was still fresh. Loss does not wait until you are ready. It asks you to keep moving while carrying something heavy inside.

When Ms. Lottie was celebrated at her homegoing service in early 2019, the church gathered as it had for generations. The sanctuary was full, and people moved freely through the aisles, embracing one another without hesitation. Friends and family came forward to hug Tameka, hold her hands, and share memories of the woman who had shaped so many lives. Grief during that season was carried through touch, presence, and the reminder that love does not end when a life does.

On Christmas Eve in 2021, Tameka and I visited my mother. She lived in the same senior complex where Tameka's mother had once lived, only one floor apart. At the time, it seemed like a small detail. Later, it became something I noticed differently.

We brought a gift we hoped would make her smile. I had ordered pillows printed with photographs of her children and grandchildren, carefully selecting each image. When we entered her apartment, something immediately felt different. The room carried a quietness that felt unnatural. My mother sat in her chair, present but silent.

I leaned close and greeted her, letting her know we were there, but she did not respond. Tameka and I sat beside her, showing her the pictures and telling her how much we loved her while her caregiver moved gently through the room with the calm steadiness of someone familiar with moments like these.

Before we left, the caregiver quietly pulled me aside and explained that she had seen this kind of silence before and that, in her experience, it often meant the end was near. Her words did not interrupt the moment as much as they gave shape to what I had already begun to feel but had not yet allowed myself to say aloud.

We hugged my mother, told her we loved her, and walked down the hallway together. The elevator ride was quiet, and when we stepped outside into the night, there was little left to say. Years later, I still recognize that evening not simply as silence, but as a kind of closing.

Five days later, early on the morning of December 29, 2021, the phone rang again. This time, my sister Diane's name appeared on the screen. When I answered, she told me our mother was gone, and in that moment, the weight shifted. This time, Tameka steadied me.

The drive that followed felt different from the one we had taken two years earlier. I sat in the passenger seat while she drove, and the same roads that had once carried her grief now carried mine. The silence between us felt familiar, but the weight had changed. I was no longer the one trying to hold everything together. I was the one being carried.

She did not try to fill the silence with explanations or rushed comfort. She simply remained present, just as I had tried to remain present for her. What we had learned during earlier seasons of our marriage showed up naturally, not as something forced, but as something that had slowly become part of who we were together. The honesty, patience, understanding, and willingness to remain present that had been forged through rebuilding, recovery, and years of learning to love differently were now serving us in a very different season.

There was no discussion about roles and no need to assign strength. When her mother passed, I carried what I could so she could grieve. When mine passed, she carried what I no longer had the strength to hold alone. Years earlier, we might not have known how to do that for one another. By then, it had become part of who we were. The exchange was never planned. It was simply lived.

Once again, arrangements had to be made. The same kinds of phone calls returned, and the same difficult decisions had to be handled, but this time it was my loss, and I was not carrying it by myself.

When my mother was celebrated at her homegoing service in early 2022, the world had already changed. COVID had reshaped how people gathered, even in grief. The sanctuary still held love, but it looked different. Space separated people who normally would have sat close together, and comfort was expressed with distance rather than touch. The affection had not disappeared, but the way it was expressed had changed.

Both services were filled with love, though they unfolded under very different circumstances. One allowed physical closeness, while the other required visible restraint. Yet in both moments, something steady remained.

During that season, no explanations could lift the weight of what we were experiencing. What remained was presence. It appeared in quiet ways: sitting beside one another, walking through difficult spaces together, and sharing silence when words were no longer enough.

Earlier in our marriage, we faced a different kind of test, one that exposed our weaknesses and required rebuilding. This season was different. It did not expose something broken between us. It revealed what we had learned how to carry together.

We did not grieve in the same way, and we did not need to. Her grief carried the shock of sudden loss, while mine carried the slow awareness that had been building over time. Neither experience was greater than the other. Both required patience, presence, and understanding.

What became clearest during that season was not how strong we were individually, but how we had learned to remain with one another when life became heavy.

Two calls entered our lives carrying finality. Two car rides held words neither of us wanted to hear. In both moments, we found ourselves doing for each other what earlier years of our marriage had prepared us to do.

The pain did not lessen because we understood it, and it did not disappear because we were somehow prepared for it. What had changed was that neither of us carried it alone. The years had taught us how to remain present with one another, and in those difficult seasons, we discovered that becoming one was about more than sharing joy, rebuilding trust, or learning to love differently. It was also about learning how to carry one another through grief.

Conclusion: Becoming One, Still Becoming

When I think about our marriage now, the word that comes to mind is steadiness. It is not the effortless closeness of our early years, nor is it the careful rebuilding that followed the most difficult seasons of our relationship. What we live in now feels quieter than either of those seasons, but it also feels stronger. The life we share today was not built in a single moment. It was formed through years of ordinary days, difficult conversations, unexpected challenges, personal growth, and the ongoing decision to remain committed to one another.

Our mornings often begin the same way. We prepare lunches for work, move through familiar routines, and cross paths throughout the house as each of us gets ready for the day. Tameka usually heads upstairs to work out in our home gym while I go downstairs to my office to do the same. Later, we find ourselves back in the bedroom getting dressed for work, picking up conversations that may have started earlier that morning. Those conversations often continue in the car as we drive to work together. Some mornings, we talk the entire ride. Other mornings we listen to music, sing along with songs we both know, and enjoy the quiet. Neither of us feels pressured to fill every moment with words because silence no longer feels uncertain. It feels familiar.

We still disagree from time to time. We still misunderstand one another occasionally. We still have moments when one of us becomes frustrated or when life places pressures on us that neither of us anticipated. The difference is not that those things have disappeared. The difference is in how we respond to them. Earlier in our marriage, tension sometimes created distance. Today, we tend to move toward the conversation rather than away from it. We have learned that understanding does not always happen immediately and that some things require patience. We have also learned that neither of us is responsible for managing the other person. Each of us must take responsibility for our own thoughts, actions, attitudes, and growth.

That lesson became one of the most important gifts to emerge from the years described in this book. For a long time, I viewed many of life's challenges through the lens of circumstances and other people. Recovery forced me to look inward in ways I never had before. It required me to stop focusing on what others were doing and begin examining what was happening within me. At the same time, our marriage continued developing in ways neither of us could have predicted. The conversations we were having, the honesty we were practicing, and the changes taking place in our relationship gradually created a different kind of closeness than the one we had experienced during the earlier years of our marriage.

Looking back now, I can see that the work was never limited to restoring trust. Trust mattered, but something larger was happening. We were learning how to relate to one another differently. We were learning to listen without immediately defending ourselves, to speak honestly without fear, and to allow room for growth without demanding perfection. The process did not make either of us flawless. If anything, it made us more aware of our imperfections. At the same time, it helped us stop expecting from each other what only GOD could provide. That shift affected almost every part of our marriage, including the way we communicated, handled conflict, approached disappointment, and viewed ourselves. The years that followed exposure, recovery, and rebuilding were not simply years of repairing damage. These were years of becoming different people than we had been before.

One of those changes can be seen in something as simple as a single word. For years, Tameka and I had told each other, "I love you." Those words mattered, but one day she added the word "more," and somehow it carried a different weight. "I love you more" was no longer simply an expression of affection. It reflected everything we had walked through together. It carried memories of difficult conversations, painful truths, patient rebuilding, seasons of grief, and the work of recovery that reshaped both our marriage and our lives. The framed picture hanging above my dresser serves as a daily reminder of all those years. Every time I see it, I am reminded that love is not something that remains unchanged. It grows, deepens, stretches, and matures as two people continue walking through life together.

My mother often said that the blessing is in the cleanup. Growing up, I thought she was talking about chores, responsibility, and keeping a house in order. Over the years,

I came to see that her words reached far beyond that. Every relationship eventually encounters things that must be addressed rather than ignored. Every person accumulates habits, wounds, assumptions, fears, and failures that cannot remain hidden forever. The cleanup is not always dramatic. More often, it happens through conversations, apologies, forgiveness, accountability, honesty, and the willingness to keep showing up even when the process feels uncomfortable. Much of what we enjoy today was built during those seasons when something needed to be faced rather than avoided.

When I look back over the story I have shared in these pages, I do not see a straight line. I see moments of joy, seasons of confusion, failures, victories, grief, growth, setbacks, recovery, and grace. I see a young couple who believed love alone would be enough. I see a husband who knew far more theology than he knew about himself. I see a wife whose strength often showed in ways easy to overlook. I see two people learning lessons neither of them expected to learn when they exchanged vows. Most of all, I see the faithfulness of GOD working through situations that often felt far beyond our ability to manage.

Looking back, I can also see that GOD was doing something in my life that extended beyond my marriage. The journey that led me into recovery also led me into journaling. What began as a way of processing thoughts, emotions, struggles, and growth gradually became something more. Through the discipline of writing things down, I found myself paying closer attention to what GOD was teaching me, what He was revealing within me, and how He was working through experiences I once wished had never happened.

Over time, journaling became writing, and writing became one of the places where I sensed GOD's direction most clearly. What began as a tool for healing became a way to reflect, learn, teach, and share what GOD had done in my life. Looking back now, I can see connections that were invisible to me. Recovery did not simply help save my marriage. It also helped lead me toward a calling I did not fully recognize at the time. In ways I could never have anticipated, some of the most difficult seasons of my life helped prepare me for the work I am doing now.

The marriage we have today is not something we created through our own wisdom or strength. It has been shaped through years of grace operating in places where neither of us recognized it at the time. There were seasons when I thought the story was primarily about failure. There were seasons when I thought it was primarily about survival. Looking back now, I believe it is ultimately a story about transformation. Not instant transformation, but the slow work that takes place when truth is faced honestly, and grace is allowed to do what effort alone cannot accomplish.

Becoming one did not happen completely on our wedding day, and it did not end once the crisis passed. It has continued through every season that followed. It continues in the conversations we have today, the choices we make, the ways we care for one another, and the life we continue building together. The covenant we entered years ago is still shaping us, and in many ways, we are still growing into it.

After all these years, we are still becoming.

When I Finished Writing, I Found This

After finishing the book—after multiple read-throughs and making the necessary corrections—I was preparing to give the manuscript to Tameka the next day so she could read it and begin working on the Foreword.

That evening, while looking through a few books on my bookshelf and studying how other authors designed their chapter headers, I opened one, and something immediately caught my attention. Inside, I found an anniversary card that Tameka had given me a couple of years after the fire.

The front of the card read, *"For the One I Love."*

Inside were the printed words:

"I love you not only for who you are, but for all we've been through together. We've shared a lot of good times, and some hard times too. But no matter what has come our way, we've always known that with God and each other, we could make it through."

For a moment, I stood there holding the card. Then I opened it fully. At the top of the inside page was a Scripture reference:

7 Many waters cannot quench love; rivers cannot wash it away.
Song of Solomon 8:7 (NIV)

Beneath it, she had written my name, followed by her own words:

"So here we are, with a love that's stronger and a faith that's deeper than the day we said, 'I do.' I'm thankful for that, and even more thankful for you—the one I will always love."

Below that were the printed words, Happy 4th Anniversary, and then she signed it simply:

"Love,
Your Wife,
Tameka Hudson"

I stood there quietly, reading it again, letting the weight of it settle in.

Finding that card did not change the story I had just written. The story was already complete. Every chapter, every moment, every season had already been laid out on the page.

But it did something else.

It reminded me that long before I fully understood what was happening within me, Tameka was already seeing our marriage through a different lens. While I was focused on surviving difficult seasons, she was recognizing the faithfulness of GOD within them. While I was still learning what covenant required, she was already holding on to the belief that what GOD had joined together was worth fighting for.

Reading her words years later, after finishing this manuscript, felt less like finding an old anniversary card and more like discovering a piece of our story that had been waiting for me all along. The love she described was not a perfect love. It had already survived disappointment, misunderstanding, rebuilding, and hard conversations. Even then, she saw a love growing stronger and a faith deepening.

By the time I found that card, I realized she had been describing the very story I had just finished writing.

Perhaps that is why Song of Solomon 8:7 was written at the top of the page:

"Many waters cannot quench love; rivers cannot sweep it away."

Looking back now, I understand that the waters were real. The struggles were real. The failures were real. Yet by the grace of GOD, they were not stronger than the covenant we made, the work GOD was doing within us, or the love that continued growing through every season we walked through together.

In many ways, that card says in a few sentences what this entire book has been trying to say in many pages.

Acknowledgments & Credits

Before I thank anyone else, I must begin with my wife, Tameka. She is my wife, my life partner, my closest friend, and the woman who has shared the journey of building a home, raising our children, and walking through every season of our marriage together. The story told in these pages is not simply mine. It is ours.

Thank you for standing with me through the easy seasons and the difficult seasons. Thank you for your patience, your strength, and your willingness to continue building with me even when the road required faith, forgiveness, and perseverance.

I am also deeply grateful that you agreed to write the Foreword for this book. Your voice brings honesty, wisdom, and perspective to this story in a way that only you can. Your words remind readers that what GOD preserved between us was not just a marriage, but a covenant.

To my children, you are the fruit of this legacy. I pray these pages bless and guide you for years to come.

Christian, as my oldest, you hold a special place in our family's story. I have watched you grow with strength, resilience, and a steady spirit. My prayer is that you continue to walk in wisdom, confidence, and faith. May you carry forward the lessons of love, perseverance, and grace, and may GOD guide your steps in every season of your life.

Angelica "Luka," you will always be my child, and my love for you has never been defined by distance, silence, or difference. It is constant. I pray that wherever life takes you, you will know that you are deeply loved, and that GOD's hand is still upon your life. My hope is that these words reach you in a way my voice sometimes cannot.

Mayuni, your strength, spirit, and presence have always brought a unique light into our family. I pray that you continue to grow in confidence, wisdom, and purpose. May you always know your value, walk in truth, and never lose the joy and depth that make you who you are.

Riakeye, you have brought so much joy and life into our family. Watching you grow has been a reminder of GOD's continued grace and blessing. I pray that you walk boldly in who you are, grounded in faith and guided by wisdom as you continue to grow into the person GOD has called you to be.

To my mother, Alice Hayes Hudson, thank you for the life you lived before me and the lessons you poured into me every single day. You did not just teach with words. You taught through your hands, your routines, your discipline, and your consistency. Through you, I learned that how we live matters, that order reflects character, and that faith is something we practice, not just something we say.

The standards you held and the example you set stayed with me far beyond childhood. I now understand that what you were building in me was not just a habit, but a foundation. Everything I have written, and everything I strive to be, carries your imprint. I am grateful for you, I honor you, and I thank GOD for choosing you to be my mother.

To Lottie Francis, who has taken her eternal rest, thank you for loving me, supporting me, and standing with me during one of the most difficult seasons of my life. When I made mistakes that could have cost me everything, your grace did not turn away from me. Instead, it helped carry me through.

Your wisdom, strength, and compassion left a lasting impact on me, and I will never forget what you meant to me.

To my father, Earlie Amis Hudson Sr., thank you for teaching me what it means to be a man. Through your life and example, you showed me strength, responsibility, and perseverance. The lessons you gave me continue to shape who I am today.

To stepmom Diane Amis, the best stepmom anyone could ask for, thank you for loving me as if you had given birth to me. You stepped into my life with care, patience, and a genuine heart, and you never made me feel like anything less than your own. That kind of love is a gift, and I do not take it for granted. Your presence has been a blessing in my life, and I am grateful for the role you have played in shaping who I am.

To my sister, Linda Copeland, who has taken her eternal rest, you were truly the best big sister I could have ever asked for. You were more than a sister to me. You were like a second mother. I remember when I was young, you would make me a red velvet cake for my birthday every year. That may seem simple, but it meant everything. It was your way of showing love, and I felt it.

To my sister, Freda "Diane" Hudson: Thanks for all the lessons you taught me as a child. I will never forget one of those lessons: "Just because you can see what people have, don't see what they have to do to keep what they have."

You represented what family looks like at its best. As a wife, a mother, a grandmother, and a mother-in-law, you created a home that reflected love, care, and togetherness. You did not just talk about family. You lived it.

You were also a great friend to Tameka, and that meant more than I can express. You embraced her with genuine love, and that bond strengthened all of us.

Your life, your love, and your example continue to live on in me. I honor you, I miss you, and I thank GOD for the gift of having you as my sister.

To my brother, William Hudson, who has also taken his eternal rest, you were more than a brother. Growing up, you helped guide and discipline me, and even as an adult, you never stopped speaking into my life. Your favorite saying, "Winners always win!" still echoes in my mind. I still listen to your old messages from time to time.

To my brother, Victor "Gene" Hudson, thank you for loving me without pressure or expectations. You have always been a quiet strength in my life. And to your wife, Celita, thank you for the love and friendship you have shown our family.

To Pastor Maynon Copeland, thank you for loving my sister faithfully and standing beside her throughout her illness. Your example is one I will never forget.

To Henry Francis, thank you for being such a wonderful father-in-law, sports buddy, and friend. Our conversations, laughter, and shared moments have been a gift to me.

To Subrena and Keasha, thank you for a bond that has always felt more like that of siblings than of a niece and an uncle.

To Alexander, Bridgett, Nylous, and Eric, thank you for the laughs, lessons, and love we shared growing up.

To Pastor David Roy, my first spiritual advisor, thank you for opening the world of biblical learning to me and planting within me a hunger for the Word of GOD.

To all my family, my wife's family, and my stepmom's family, thank you for the blessings, encouragement, and love you have poured into my life.

I also want to express gratitude to the Respiratory Therapy Department at Georgia State University, including Dr. and Mrs. Rau, Dr. Goodfellow, Dr. Deshpande, Dr. Martin, Dr. Petty, and Kristy. Your support and kindness during an important season of our lives meant more than you know.

Meryl, thank you for being our wedding photographer and capturing memories we still cherish today.

I also want to thank our college technology team. Al, thank you for first giving me an opportunity as a student assistant and later hiring me full-time. Tiffany, thank you for teaching me the foundations of technical support. Herb, your dependability and focus have always inspired me. Alonzo, thank you for your commitment and consistency.

To Anthony, thank you for recognizing my potential and entrusting me with leadership responsibilities for more than two decades. To Dean Mo and Dr. Nucci, thank you for your humility, patience, encouragement, and leadership.

To Vanessa, thank you for your kindness, support, and friendship to both Tameka and our family throughout the years.

And to Douglass High, Class of 1990, thank you for the friendships and sense of community that continue to surround our family today.

Finally, I want to thank ChatGPT, an OpenAI product, for providing thoughtful assistance throughout the writing of this book. Its support with editing, organization, formatting, and scriptural reflections helped shape this manuscript with clarity and care. All final content, interpretations, and perspectives remain entirely my own.

Up Next:

THE BLESSING IS IN THE CLEANUP

Order, Responsibility, and Redemption

Made in the USA
Coppell, TX
20 June 2026

82574199R00073